Visiting the Vet

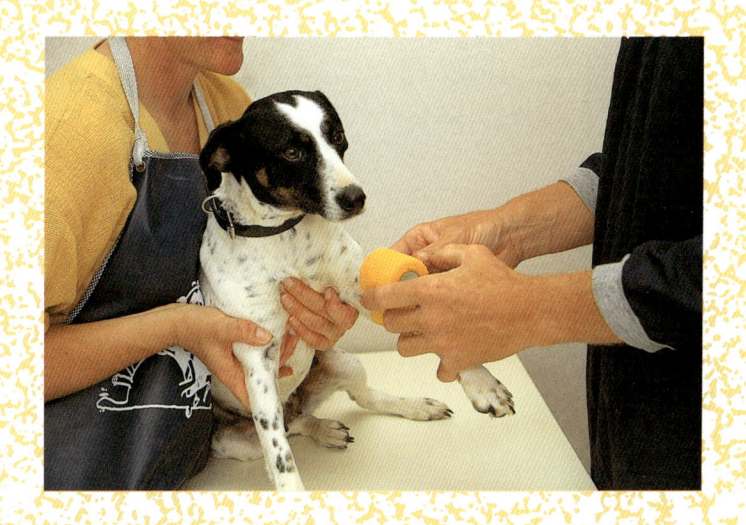

By Graham Meadows

It is Monday morning at school.
Today some of the children
are going to visit the veterinarian.

The children get on the bus.
They are all excited.

The bus sets off.

The bus arrives at the vet's. One of the vets comes out to meet the children.
"My name is Kathy," she says.

"I am going to show you around."

The children go into a waiting room. "Who's that sitting behind the desk?" says Amy.

"That's Myra," says Kathy.
"She's our secretary."

Myra smiles.
"When a person brings in an animal,
I put the animal's name on the computer.
Each animal has its own file."

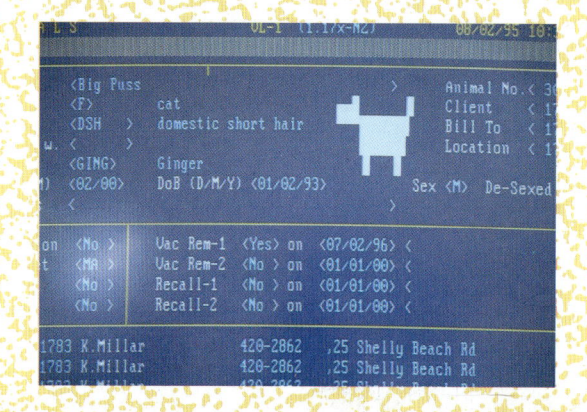

She points to the waiting room. "People and animals can sit here until it's their turn to see the vet."

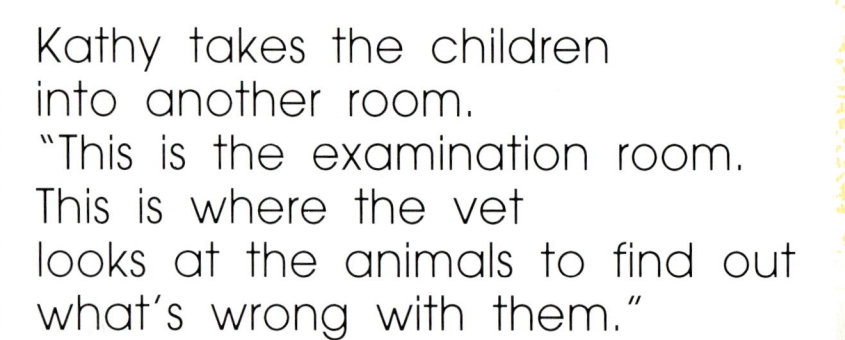

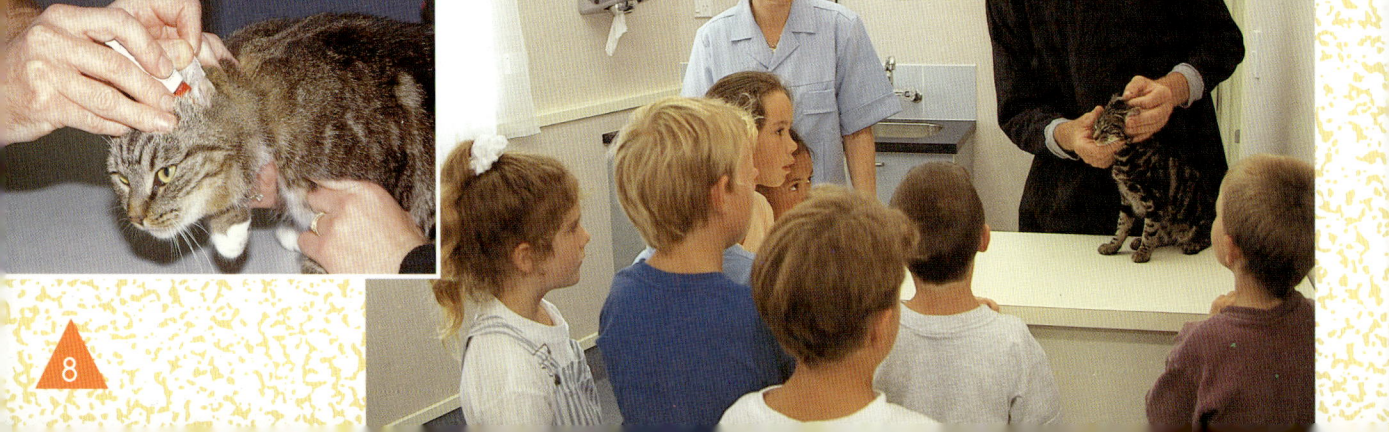

Kathy takes the children
into another room.
"This is the examination room.
This is where the vet
looks at the animals to find out
what's wrong with them."

Then the children go into the recovery room.

"This is where the animals get better after an operation," says Kathy.

"Where are the animals now?" says Amy.
Kathy takes the children
to two rooms out in the back.
One has small cages
for the small animals.
The other has big cages
for the bigger animals.

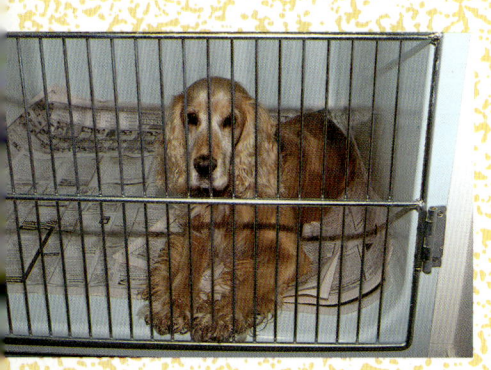

"Are these animals sick?"
says Jason.

"Yes," says Kathy.
"They have to stay here
until the vet says they can go home."

"You have to go now,"
says Kathy.
"The bus is waiting for you."

"I think I want to be a vet,"
says Amy as they climb on the bus.